303.4833
Lester
2011

D0914963

WITHDRAWN

R U In?

Using Technology Responsibly

ABDO
Publishing Company

A GUY'S GUIDE

R U In?

Using Technology Responsibly

by Brian Lester

Content Consultant
Dr. Robyn J. A. Silverman
Child/Teen Development Expert and Success Coach
Powerful Words Character Development

Credits

Published by ABDO Publishing Company, 8000 West 78th Street, Edina, Minnesota 55439. Copyright © 2011 by Abdo Consulting Group, Inc. International copyrights reserved in all countries. No part of this book may be reproduced in any form without written permission from the publisher. The Essential Library™ is a trademark and logo of ABDO Publishing Company.

Printed in the United States of America,
North Mankato, Minnesota
062010
092010

 THIS BOOK CONTAINS AT LEAST 10% RECYCLED MATERIALS.

Editor: Mari Kesselring
Copy Editor: Nicholas Cafarelli
Interior Design and Production: Kazuko Collins
Cover Design: Marie Tupy

Library of Congress Cataloging-in-Publication Data
Lester, Brian, 1975-
  R U in? : using technology responsibly / Brian Lester.
     p. cm.
  ISBN 978-1-61613-543-0
  1. Internet—Moral and ethical aspects—Juvenile literature. 2. Information technology—Moral and ethical aspects—Juvenile literature. 3. Online etiquette—Juvenile literature. 4. Internet—Social aspects—Juvenile literature. 5. Responsibility—Juvenile literature. I. Title. II. Title: Are you in?
  TK5105.878.L47 2011
  303.48'33--dc22
                                        2010017024

contents

Meet Dr. Robyn 6

Take It from Me 8

Chapter 1. The Texting Cheater 10

Chapter 2. The Gamer 20

Chapter 3. Gotta Have It 30

Chapter 4. Online Life. 40

Chapter 5. Close Call 48

Chapter 6. Overexposed. 58

Chapter 7. Left Out 66

Chapter 8. Cyberbully 76

Chapter 9. Stuntman 86

Chapter 10. Public Matter 94

A Second Look 102

Pay It Forward. 104

Additional Resources 106

Glossary. 108

Index 110

About the Author. 112

Dr. Robyn Silverman truly enjoys spending time with young people. In fact, it's what she does best! As a child and teen development specialist, Dr. Robyn has devoted her career to helping guys just like you become all they can be—and possibly more than they ever imagined. Throughout this series, you'll read her expert advice on friends, girls, classmates, school, family, and everything in between.

A self-esteem and body image expert, Dr. Robyn takes a positive approach to life. She knows how tough it is to be a kid in today's world, and she's prepared with encouragement and guidance to help you become your very best and realize your goals.

Dr. Robyn helps young people share their wildest dreams and biggest problems. Her compassion, openness, and honesty make her trusted by many adolescents, and she considers it a gift to be able to interact with the young people whom she sees as the leaders of tomorrow. She created the Powerful Words Character Development system, a program taught all over the world in martial arts and other sports programs to help guys just like you become examples to others in their communities.

As a speaker, success coach, and award-winning author, Dr. Robyn's powerful messages have reached thousands of people. Her expert advice has been featured in *Prevention* magazine, *Parenting* magazine, *U.S. News and World Report*, and the *Washington Post*. She was an expert for *The Tyra Show, Fox News,* and NBC's *LXtv.* She has an online presence, too. You can follow her on Twitter, become a fan on Facebook, and read her blog on her Web site, www.DrRobynSilverman.com. When she isn't working, Dr. Robyn enjoys spending time with her family in New Jersey.

Dr. Robyn believes that young people are assets to be developed, not problems to be fixed. As she puts it, "Guys are so much more than the way the media paints them. They have so many things to offer. I'm ready to highlight how guys get it right and tips for the ways they can make their teen years the best years so far . . . I'd be grateful if you'd come along for the ride."

Do you have a cell phone? How often do you use it to make a call or send a text? Do you have a computer? How much time do you spend on the Internet? Do you have a Facebook profile or a Twitter account? Technology is all around us. In this book, I have hit on several different aspects of technology, indicating the positives and negatives those tools can have on your life.

Chances are you use at least one form of technology every day. I use the Internet when I work as a beat writer for a small-college basketball team. It allows me to post live updates during games and get a recap online immediately after the game ends. I also use a cell phone to keep in contact with my family and help me in case of an emergency. What forms of technology do you use every day?

With the world around you changing, odds are you will one day have a job that requires using some form of technology. Keep in mind, though, that while it is important to understand technology, it can have a negative impact on your life if used the wrong way. Don't let technology consume your life. You don't want to spend so much time using high-tech gadgets that it isolates you from society. It is important to take a break each day, unplug, and get out in the real, 3-D world, and play a sport or spend quality time with your family and friends.

Technology isn't going away. It will continue to evolve, and there will always be advantages and disadvantages to it. The best advice I can give you is to never let technology replace your ability to use your mind. Always think before you act. Communication through texting or the Internet will never take the place of actual face time with people who care about you. If you take my advice, technology will be beneficial to you now and in the future.

TTYL,

Brian

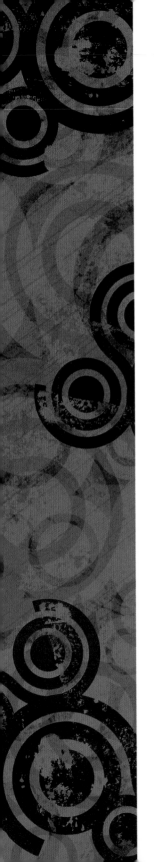

1

The Texting Cheater

Do most of your friends have cell phones? Do you? A lot of parents buy their kids cell phones to stay in touch during the day. But cell phones are also for texting and calling friends, right? They're for taking photos, recording videos, and hearing your favorite song. Texting, especially, is so convenient. You can text a quick message to your friend and receive a reply in seconds.

Your school probably has rules about when students can use their cell phones. You might be allowed to use your phone between classes or only before and after school. You might be able to carry your phone with you all day or you might have to keep it in your locker until the last bell rings. While it can be frustrating to be disconnected from your cell phone during the school day, principals and teachers have good reasons for these rules. Cell phones can be distracting when you're trying to focus on learning something new. Some kids might even use their cell phones to cheat during a test by using the Internet to look up answers or storing the answers on their phones prior to the test. Xavier made a bad choice about cell phone use. In the end, he discovered that taking the easy way out resulted in some major consequences.

Xavier's Story

Texting, especially, is so convenient. You can text a quick message to your friend and receive a reply in seconds.

On a warm spring evening, Xavier came home from playing basketball with some friends at the park. It was about 9:30, and he felt great. His team had won most of the games that night. But when Xavier walked into his bedroom and saw his history textbooks waiting on his desk, his stomach dropped. He had completely forgotten about tomorrow's big test.

Xavier threw his basketball into the closet and snatched his history book from his desk. He sat on his bed and started to frantically look through the pages. He had failed the last two tests. He knew he would do better if he had set aside time to study, but

the weather had been so nice lately, the last thing he wanted to do was sit inside with a pile of books. Xavier knew he *had* to pass this test.

He tried to memorize the facts and dates he was reading. But it seemed that no matter how hard he tried, he couldn't keep the stuff in his head. It was late, and he was so tired from playing basketball. Xavier punched his pillow as hard as he could. He was going to fail for sure.

Then Xavier noticed his cell phone sitting on the nightstand. It would be so easy just to put the answers into his phone and then look them up during the test. Students at Xavier's school were allowed to keep their phones with them during the day, but they weren't allowed to use them during class. He knew it was a risky move, but he was desperate. Xavier started typing. . . .

Think About It

- Did you ever take the easy way out, knowing it was the wrong thing to do? Were you caught? If not, did you feel bad that you got away with it?

- How far in advance do you study for a difficult test?

- Is there ever a time where you can use your cell phone appropriately in class?

The next day at school, Xavier was nervous when he got to his history class for the test. He sat down at his desk and tried to ignore the slightly sick feeling in his stomach. He hid his phone in the front pocket of his hoodie sweatshirt while Ms. Meyer passed out the tests.

At first, it wasn't easy trying to scroll through his text messages and read the answers without getting caught. But soon, Xavier was breezing through the test. When he was finished, he slipped his cell phone back into his pocket and turned in his test.

The next day in history class, Ms. Meyer smiled as she handed back Xavier's test. He got an A. Xavier had never received an A on a test before.

"Looks like all that studying is paying off!" Ms. Meyer said. Xavier tried to smile but his stomach dropped. He knew he hadn't earned his grade honestly on this test.

That day at lunch the guys were giving Xavier a hard time about his score on the test. They had all been playing basketball the night before too, and none of them had done very well on the test.

"Dude," said Tyler, "That test was insane. How'd you get an A?"

Xavier hesitated. He wasn't sure what his friends would think of him cheating, especially when they had all received such low scores.

"Come on, man," said Dan. "We know you didn't study. You must have cheated."

"I just did it once," Xavier mumbled.

Tyler looked surprised. "I hope you get caught. Seriously. I studied until midnight last night!"

"Whatever," said Dan. "Those history tests are stupid. I'm sick of studying for them and failing. And, there's another test next week. How did you do it?"

Think About It

- Have you ever worried about what your friends would think of something you did? Why were you worried?

- Why do you think Xavier's friends gave him a hard time about his score on the test?

Xavier explained to his friends how he had used his cell phone to cheat.

"That's stupid," Tyler said right away. "I can't believe she didn't catch you."

"I'm trying it on the test next week," Dan announced and turned to Xavier, "You in?"

"Okay," Xavier said. He didn't really want to cheat again. But it didn't feel right to let Dan do it alone, especially when it was Xavier's idea in the first place.

The next week, Xavier, along with a few of his friends, took out their cell phones when it was time for the history test. After Xavier told Dan his method, a few other kids had heard about it. They wanted to try it out, too. Xavier had to admit it was

pretty cool that they all thought he'd had a good idea. Still, Xavier did feel a little bit nervous to try cheating again.

When class was about halfway over, Xavier was almost finished with his test. It looked like a score for him and his friends. But then, all of a sudden, a shadow was cast over Xavier's desk. He looked up. Ms. Meyer was standing over him. She was looking at the cell phone in his hand.

"Why do you have your phone out, Xavier?" asked Ms. Meyer.

Xavier didn't know what to say. He saw the other kids who had been cheating quickly conceal

their cell phones in their hoodie pockets and up
their sleeves.

"Hand it over," Ms. Meyer said. She took
Xavier's phone, threw his test in the trash, and
escorted him to the principal's office.

The principal gave Xavier detention and called
his parents. Ms. Meyer told him he'd receive a zero
on the test and would have to come in for extra help
after school if he didn't want to fail the class. Worst
of all, the principal decided to change the school's cell
phone policy. Now no one could carry a cell phone
during the day.

"It only takes one person to ruin the privilege
for the group," said Xavier's principal. Xavier
couldn't believe what his actions had caused.

Think About It

- Have you ever been caught cheating on a test?
  How did you feel afterward?

- Do you think Xavier's punishment is fair? What
  do you think his friends' reactions will be?

- What privileges do you have at your school?
  How would you feel if you lost a privilege
  because you or someone else broke the rules?

It is convenient to have a cell phone at school so you can call your parents to pick you up after basketball practice or debate meets. It's also a fun way to keep in touch with friends. But cell phones can be a big distraction. You might have a few friends who have had their phones stolen at school or taken away by teachers. And some students, like Xavier, might even use their phones to cheat.

It might be tempting to use your cell phone during class. With so much going on in your life, you too may be tempted to cheat on a test at some point. Remind yourself that having a cell phone is a privilege. If you use it for the wrong things or at the wrong time, that privilege can be taken away and compromise the trust people have in you now and in the future.

Work It Out

1. Make sure you know what your school's policy is on cell phones. You don't want to risk losing your cell phone.

2. If you're allowed to have a cell phone at school, make sure you follow the school's rules for when it can and cannot be used. In general, turn it off or keep it on "silent"

during class. Sending texts during the day will just distract you from learning. It is also unfair to your teachers, who are working hard to teach.

3. Don't use your cell phone to cheat. Study for a test the right way. Learning the information is the ultimate goal—and cheating doesn't help you learn. If you have a hard time understanding a subject, talk to a teacher or parent so they can help you or get you a tutor.

4. Cell phones can come in handy in a variety of situations, but almost all phone calls or text messages can wait until school is over for the day.

The Last Word from Brian

Cell phones are great for communication, and texting can be really fun and helpful, too. I use my cell phone to keep in touch with friends and family when I'm on the go. But using your cell phone to cheat just isn't cool. You put yourself at risk of getting caught and, even if you get away with it, you have compromised your personal integrity. No one likes a cheater.

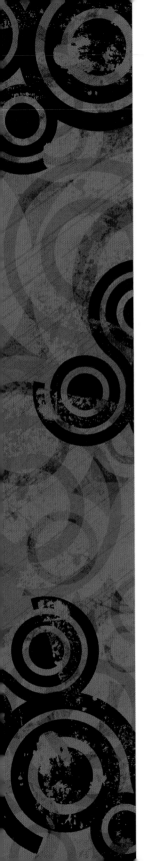

2
The Gamer

Your parents have probably told you stories about when they were your age and how their free time was spent on games of baseball in sandlots or running around the neighborhood playing a game of tag. Today, you probably have access to high-tech tools such as computers, cell phones, MP3 players, or gaming systems. You might hang out with your friends, just watching movies or playing video games. You might even play games on the Internet with your friends who live across town, while staying in your own home.

Technology has a role in pushing our world forward, but at the same time, the negatives can be huge. If you spend too much time playing video games, you won't get the amount of exercise you need. This can lead to health problems later in your life. You might also get a little too involved in a video game and forget about hanging out with your family and friends. If you play video games with violent and graphic content all of the time, you might start to act violently in some situations. Noah loved playing all kinds of video games. But he had to learn the hard way that violent video games could affect his behavior.

> If you play video games with violent and graphic content all of the time, you might start to act violently in some situations.

Noah's Story

Noah had enjoyed playing video games for almost as long as he could remember. He liked to play them alone or with a few of his friends. Noah and his friends liked to compete to see who could beat a game the quickest. He almost always won these contests.

A few years ago, Noah's parents had started to buy him more mature video games when he asked for them. These games were often rated AO for Adults Only, but they were the same games that Noah's friends were playing. Most of them involved shooting at people, and there was lots of blood and guts. Noah thought it was cool how realistic some of the graphics looked.

For his birthday, Noah got a new game, *Zombie Killer*. It had just been released, and Noah loved it. Awesome action, amazing graphics—the game had everything. Like he usually did after he got a new game, Noah would rush home every day after school, throw down his backpack, and run into his bedroom to play the game.

One day after school, he was just about to press start on the game when his mother came into his room.

"Got any homework today?" she asked.

"Yeah," Noah answered reluctantly.

"I think you should do your homework before you play your game," his mother said.

Noah groaned.

Within an hour, Noah had whipped through his homework and was finally able to play his game. He was in the middle of the game when his little brother Robert walked into his room. Robert was seven years younger than Noah, and he was always interested in whatever Noah was doing. Most of the time Noah and Robert got along, but Noah really wanted to pass level five and Robert was just a distraction.

Before Robert even had a chance to bother him, Noah yelled, "Get out of here! Can't you see I'm busy?" Robert stomped out of Noah's room, slamming the door after him.

Think About It

- Have you ever put a game you enjoyed above more important things in life?

- Has something you do for fun ever hurt your relationship with a family member?

- Do you play games that are labeled "Adults Only"?

At school the next day, Noah talked to his friends about *Zombie Killer.*

"Last night I got all the way to level five. It was so awesome," Noah said.

Noah's friend Rex laughed and started bragging, "Whatever. On my first night, I got to level seven!"

Noah suddenly felt very angry. He hated it when Rex bragged. "You're not that good. I'm going to beat the game before you will," Noah shot back.

"Yeah right! You suck!" Rex yelled.

Noah was furious. He couldn't believe Rex would yell at him in front of everyone. He was such a jerk. Frustrated, Noah lunged forward and pushed Rex to the ground. Rex jumped back up and punched Noah. Pretty soon teachers were taking them both to the principal's office.

When Noah got home from school that day, his mother sent him to his room for the night. She even took away his *Zombie Killer* game, so he couldn't play it. Instead, he had to just sit there.

Think About It

- Have you ever argued with your friends over a video game?

- Have you ever hit or punched one of your friends? Why did you do it? How did you feel about it afterward?

- Why do you think Noah fought with Rex? How do you think he felt about it?

At school the next day, Noah and his friends started talking about a new game that was coming out in a few days. It was called *Duty of War,* and it was even more intense than *Zombie Killer.* A lot of the guys' parents wouldn't even let them get it. Noah told his friends that he'd be the first one to play it.

"Hey Mom! *Duty of War* comes out next week. Will you get it for me?" Noah asked that night.

"Noah, I really don't think you need a new game right now. Your behavior in school and at home hasn't earned you anything new, and especially not another game," his mom said.

Noah couldn't believe it. What was she making such a big deal about?

Frustrated, Noah lunged forward and pushed Rex to the ground.

"But Mom, I need it!" he complained. Robert came running into the kitchen to see what was happening.

"What's going on?" Robert asked.

"Nothing! Get out of here, stupid!" Noah yelled at Robert. Noah tried to push him out of the room, but he pushed too hard and Robert fell to the floor. Robert started to cry.

"Noah!" yelled his mother. "Go to your room!"

Noah stomped off to his room. He knew he was in trouble, but he didn't care. Robert got in his way all the time, and his mom didn't understand how important it was to get *Duty of War.*

Noah started playing *Zombie Killer*. After a few minutes, his mom came in. Noah wouldn't even look at her because he was so involved in the game. Noah's mother watched him play.

"Noah," she said. "This is a very violent game. Turn it off; I want to talk with you."

"Just let me get to a place where I can save it," Noah begged. "If I stop now, I'll lose everything."

Noah's mom turned off the game system. Noah glared at her as she sat down next to him.

"Honey, do you think these violent video games are affecting your real life?" she asked.

"No," Noah grumbled as he rolled his eyes.

"Do you really think you would have gotten into that fight at school or pushed your brother down before you started playing all of these? Your behavior seems really different lately."

Noah shrugged his shoulders. He knew she might be right, but he didn't want to admit it.

Finally, she shook her head and sighed, "Noah, I think we've made a big mistake in letting you play a lot of these. The games are too violent for you to handle at your age. I'm taking them away for a while."

He wasn't sure he agreed with her, but he knew he didn't have a choice anymore.

Think About It

- Do you think the games Noah was playing were affecting his behavior?

- Was it fair for Noah's mother to take away his violent video games? How would you feel if you were Noah?

There is nothing wrong with playing video games. In fact, they can be a lot of fun! But problems can arise when you play games that are very violent or when you let video games take up all your free time. Video game ratings are a good place to start when trying to determine if a game is appropriate for your age. Kids sometimes imitate in their own life some of the behavior they see in a game. So it's important not only to look at how realistic or violent a game is, but also at whether the player must injure or kill other characters to move to the next level of a game. Aggression in the player may increase as characters in the game are harmed.

Video games can also be addictive. You have to be careful to keep your love of gaming from interfering with other aspects of your life. Spending less time with friends, a slip in grades, or changes in behavior are all signs that you could have an addiction to video games. Physical problems can also arise from a video game addiction. If you feel you have a video game addiction, one of the best ways to break it is to find other activities you enjoy such as playing sports or reading a book. In some cases, you may need to seek help from a professional.

Work It Out

1. Find things to do with your free time other than playing video games. Play a sport or a board game, learn to play an instrument, or find a fun activity you can do with your family.

2. Play video games that require strategy or movement. Strategy games can be just as much fun as violent ones, and your parents are more likely to approve. There are also lots of games that require you to get up and move around to play.

3. Find an age-appropriate game to play with a sibling or a friend. This will give you a chance to interact with someone else rather than secluding yourself from others.

4. Give your body a break from gaming. Exercise every day. Shoot some hoops or play an outdoor game.

The Last Word from Brian

It's important to talk with your parents before playing a game that borders on being too violent. Let them see the game, and if they give you reasons why it's not appropriate for you to play, take their advice. And, trust your gut. If you get the feeling that a game might be too intense, you're probably right.

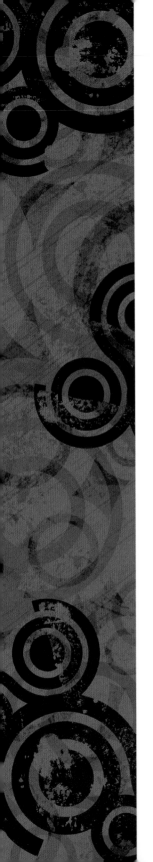

3
Gotta Have It

Do you own a lot of high-tech gadgets? Technology provides us will all kinds of cool tools. It seems as if every week there is a new cell phone, computer, video game system, or other device coming out.

If your family has the finances and the desire to do so, they might provide you with the biggest, best, and newest tech devices whenever those items are available. When a new gadget comes out, you might get it right way. But with new products coming out all the time, this can become an expensive habit. Find out how Jackson learned to appreciate the things he already had.

Jackson's Story

For as long as he could remember, Jackson always had nice things. All he had to do was ask for what he wanted, and his parents would get it for him. Jackson had a flat-screen HDTV with Blu-ray, two video game systems, and a top-of-the-line laptop in his room. He also had a cell phone with unlimited text messaging and the best iPod. Jackson even had his own video camera, so he could make movies with his friends.

It seems as if every week there is a new cell phone, computer, video game system, or other device coming out.

Jackson enjoyed all of his gadgets. It didn't matter to him if something got lost or broken because he knew his parents would replace it. He was always looking for the next cool device to get.

Think About It

- Have you ever been in a position where you get most of the things you ask for?

- Have you ever broken or lost an expensive gadget?

- Have you ever been frustrated by all the gadgets a friend gets?

One day after school, Jackson and his friend Cole walked to a tech store they both liked. Cole pointed to a poster in the front of the store as they walked in. The poster had an image of a sleek, black cell phone. It had a large touch screen. "Coming this March . . . The Blaze!" the poster read. Jackson thought the phone looked cooler than any phone he'd ever had.

"Sweet!" Jackson said. "I'm so gonna get that."

"Yeah, right," said Cole. "It's super expensive."

"My parents love that stuff," said Jackson. "They'll get it for me."

Cole shrugged his shoulders, but Jackson could tell he was jealous. Jackson would probably be the only kid at his middle school with the Blaze.

Think About It

- Was there ever an expensive device that you really wanted? Why did you want it?

- Have you ever felt happy to have things that your friends don't have?

- Do you think your friends have ever been jealous of you? Have you ever been jealous of something your friend had?

When Jackson got home, his dad had just arrived home from work. Jackson told his dad all about the Blaze and how much he wanted it.

"I don't know, Jackson," said his dad. "You don't take very good care of the things we buy for you. Plus, I thought we just bought you a new phone."

Jackson took his cell phone out of his pocket. He had really liked this phone when he got it a month ago. But the Blaze was so much cooler.

"I don't want it anymore." Jackson set the cell phone on the kitchen table. "Dad, the Blaze is so cool. I really need it!"

"I don't think so, Jackson," said his dad. "I know you get a lot of gifts from your mom and me.

He had really liked this phone when he got it a month ago. But the Blaze was so much cooler.

But I think you need to start learning to appreciate what you have."

Jackson was furious. He'd made a big deal to Cole about getting the Blaze. What would Cole say when he found out Jackson couldn't get it after all?

"This is so unfair," Jackson muttered.

"The phone we got you last month is really cool, too," his dad said. "I bet you haven't even tried out all its features yet. See if you can enjoy that phone for a while longer. Then, if you really want the Blaze, maybe you can get it for your birthday."

Jackson suppressed a groan. His birthday was still seven months away.

Think About It

- Do you think Jackson's dad is likely to change his mind about the phone? Why or why not?

- Have you ever assumed you could have something only to find out that you couldn't get it?

- Have you ever pressured your parents to buy you something?

The next day after school, Jackson and Cole met up to play catch in the park. Jackson decided not to tell Cole that his parents had said no to the Blaze. Maybe they would still change their minds.

Jackson noticed his friend Tim shooting hoops at the basketball court nearby. Tim was the captain of the basketball team. It seemed like everyone was friends with him.

"Hey Tim!" Jackson yelled. Tim waved and came running over.

"What's up?" Tim asked.

"Wanna get some pizza with us after your game?" Cole asked.

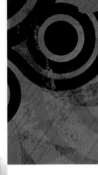

"Sure, I've gotta run home and check with my mom though," Tim said.

"Why don't you just call her?" Jackson asked.

Tim shrugged. "I don't have a cell phone. No one in my family does. We can't afford it. It's not a big deal, though."

Jackson was surprised. It seemed like everyone at school had a cell phone. And Tim really didn't seem to care. Jackson suddenly felt stupid for making such a big deal about getting the Blaze.

"You can use mine," Jackson offered. He handed his phone to Tim.

"Sweet phone!" Tim said.

"Not as cool as the one he's gonna get!" Cole exclaimed. "Jackson's getting the Blaze!"

"Wow, really?" Tim asked.

"Actually, I don't know if I can," Jackson said. Suddenly, Jackson didn't want the Blaze so much anymore. He realized he was lucky to have any phone at all.

Think About It

- Have you ever felt as if you took something you owned for granted?

- Did you ever have to wait to get something you really wanted? How did you feel when you finally got it?

- Why do you think Jackson cares less about getting the Blaze after hearing that Tim doesn't own a cell phone?

Tons of high-tech gadgets are currently marketed to you and your peers. These items can be a lot of fun to have, but they are also expensive. You might feel that having cool tech gadgets will earn you admiration from your friends. You might even feel that you need items like an MP3 player or a cell phone to fit in among your peers. But remember it is better to have people like you for your personality, like how Jackson appreciated Tim, than for what you have.

One way to break up the "gotta have it" mentality is to shift your attention to doing something generous for others. Doing something good for someone less fortunate, be it donating money to a charity, giving away old clothes or toys, or donating your time to an important cause, will help you develop an appreciation for what you do have. You will also feel better about yourself because you did something good for another person.

Work It Out

1. Take good care of the things you already own. They will last longer and your parents will see that you are responsible.

2. High-tech gadgets are expensive. Rather than ask your parents to purchase something for you, see how you can save up the money to buy it yourself.

3. If you want a high-tech device, be smart about it. Research different brands rather than automatically choosing the most popular or newest model. You can usually find the best deals on slightly older models.

4. Realize that it's more important for people to like you for who you are rather than what you have.

The Last Word from Brian

At some point, most of us have a "gotta have it" attitude about some high-tech item. It is best to realize, however, that you can't always get what you want. Sometimes you need to appreciate what you already have. If a "gotta have it" obsession gets to the point where it is changing your behavior, step back for a moment and evaluate your actions. There is nothing wrong with wanting something high tech, but just remember not to let that "want" interfere with what is really important in life. Most important, do not let your stuff define who you are.

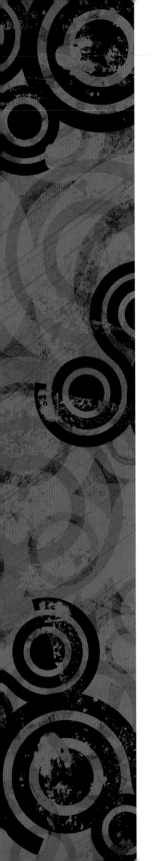

4

Online Life

Social networking has become very popular. With the emergence of Web sites such as Facebook, Twitter, MySpace, and people blogging about everything under the sun, socializing online is as common as socializing face-to-face.

There are some great things about social networking. You can become friends with anyone no matter where they live. This can put you in contact with different types of people. You might even learn about cultures different from your own. However, there are drawbacks to social-networking sites, too. Spending too much time on them can become an addiction. For some people your age, a

site like Facebook is a virtual world where you can be someone you aren't or talk about things you don't feel you can talk about in your real life. Find out how Curt learned to make friends in the world away from his computer.

Curt's Story

Curt had always been shy and rarely socialized with his classmates, but he did have a few close friends at school. Lately, though, things had changed in Curt's life. He seemed to be home more and was seeing his friends less. He started spending most of his time online. He had some friends that he talked to online but had

There are some great things about social networking. You can become friends with anyone no matter where they live.

never actually met. He just played computer games or instant messaged with them on the Internet. Curt found it a lot easier to make friends online.

One night at dinner, Curt's mother asked him if he was going to hang out with his friend Brandon after dinner.

"I don't know," Curt said. He hadn't seen Brandon in awhile.

"How come you guys don't hang out as much anymore?" his mother asked. "Did something happen?"

"No," Curt mumbled. He knew his parents didn't like him spending so much time online. They didn't understand that Curt's online friends were just like real friends.

"Basketball tryouts are this week," Curt's dad said. "How about trying out this year?"

Curt shrugged. He used to like basketball, but he knew going to practice every afternoon would take a huge amount of time. "I don't want to," he said.

He wrote an entry in his blog about how annoying his parents were.

"Is everything okay?" Curt's mother looked concerned. "I really think it would be good for you to get off the computer tonight."

Curt slammed down his fork, stood up, and shouted, "Everything is fine, okay? I just don't feel like doing anything!"

Curt ran upstairs and slammed the door of his bedroom.

Think About It

- How much time do you spend online each day? Do you think you spend more time online than you do in the "real world"?

- Do you think it is bad for you to spend a lot of your time online? why or why not?

- why do you think Curt's parents asked about Brandon and basketball tryouts?

Once in his room, Curt logged on to his computer. He wrote an entry in his blog about how annoying his parents were. Curt wrapped up the blog entry, then signed on to Facebook. He updated his status, "My life SUCKS!" Some of his friends commented immediately with responses such as "Me too!" and "I hear ya." Someone even asked, "What's wrong?"

Curt saw that his friend Adam was online. Curt met Adam when they were both playing a computer game online. Adam lived in another state but he was Curt's same age. They instant messaged each other a lot.

Curt instant messaged Adam: "Hey dude!"
To Curt's surprise an automatic away message from
Adam popped up: "Out running with Henry! Cya!"
Adam was away for the rest of the evening and Curt
was really bored. He really wished he had someone
to talk to.

At school the next day, Curt ran into Brandon.

"Hey Curt, what's up? I haven't seen you
in forever," Brandon said as they stood outside a
classroom.

"Not much, I guess," Curt said.

"You should go to basketball tryouts on Friday,"
Brandon said. "You were really solid last year."

"I guess I could at least try out," Curt said.

"Awesome!" said Brandon. "I'll see ya then."

Curt went to the tryout and had a blast. He'd forgotten how much he loved basketball. After tryouts, Brandon and a few of the other players were headed out for pizza. They invited Curt to join them.

When Curt got home that night he was too tired from tryouts and pizza with the guys to go online. Instead, he jumped right into bed.

Curt made the team, and on the days that he didn't practice, he was outside in the driveway shooting hoops with Brandon. Curt was having so much fun on the basketball team that he didn't talk to his online friends as much. One evening he signed online and Adam sent him an instant message.

"Hey! Where have u been?"

"On the basketball team," Curt wrote back.

"Awesome," Adam wrote.

Just then, Curt got a text message from Brandon: "BB practice @ park?"

Curt typed a message to Adam, "Gotta go! TTYL," and rushed off to meet Brandon.

Think About It

- Have you ever used a computer so much that you quit doing something you used to love?

- Do you feel better about yourself after participating in an activity you enjoy?

Kids who spend most of their free time on the Internet have a tendency to avoid healthy social contact. A recent study showed that children between the ages of 8 and 18 spend an average of 7 hours and 38 minutes per day using some form of technology for fun. That includes the Internet, where kids share information about themselves with their friends and even people they don't know through blogs and on social networking pages.

Communicating via the Internet can be a lot of fun, but it cannot take the place of hanging out with your friends in the real world. You might feel better posting your angry thoughts on Facebook or in your blog, but it doesn't fix the problem. Active, social hobbies that can get you out of the house and away from your computer can help you feel positive about yourself and your life, a lesson Curt learned after joining the basketball team.

Work It Out

1. Limit your time online to an hour or two a day, and don't spend all that time on social network pages. Use informational sites to learn about the world and what is happening.

2. Ask your parents to keep the computer in a room where the family usually gathers. This will help you avoid the feeling of being secluded while you are on the computer.

3. Stay involved in something that doesn't involve the cyberworld. Try playing sports or hanging out with friends.

4. If you tend to socialize primarily online because you are shy, take a step toward learning how to interact more with others. Joining a team or getting involved in a hobby with people who have similar interests will help you open up more.

The Last Word from Brian

It is so easy to share your feelings online. You can talk about the good, the bad, and the ugly without ever having to come face-to-face with someone. The drawback is that you can distance yourself from life outside the cyberworld. Getting involved in sports or another extracurricular activity can make you realize that there's a whole world beyond your computer. These types of social activities can be more difficult if you're a shy person. The best way to get over shyness and start showing the world who you are, though, is to just get out there! Don't let your shy personality hold you back from making friends and enjoying your life.

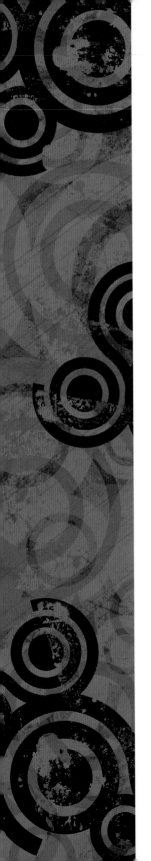

5

Close Call

C hat rooms have become a big part of the online experience. You can meet anyone from anywhere in the world. But you really don't know if the people you are chatting with are who they say they are. Some people hide behind a computer and use innocent screen names and fake profiles in an attempt to come into contact with unsuspecting people.

A 45-year-old man can tell you he is a 12-year-old girl with the same likes and dislikes as you. You may let your guard down if you believe you are talking with a girl you have a lot in common with. An online predator may be able to get personal information from you such as a phone number, the name of your school, and even your home address. See how Eli found out you can't always trust the person you are chatting with online.

Eli's Story

The sound of fingertips hitting a keyboard broke the silence of an empty living room. Eli was busy chatting online again, just as he did each day after school while waiting for his parents to come home from work. He was instant messaging with a couple of his friends from school when he decided to check out a chat room about airplanes. There were a bunch of people in the chat room. Suddenly, Eli received an instant message from Michelle44. She had been in the airplane chat room, too.

You may let your guard down if you believe you are talking with a girl you have a lot in common with.

Eli was surprised but did not hesitate to reply. He asked her age and where she was from. Michelle fired a message back that said she was 12 and from Freeport, a town just 15 minutes away from Eli.

He thought that was cool. They spent the next two hours talking. She was really into airplanes, too. She also wanted to be a pilot. Eli finally had to log off and get ready for dinner. He told her they could chat again later on. They instant messaged again the next day and followed that same pattern for about a week.

Think About It

- Do you spend time in chat rooms? If you do, who do you usually talk to?

- Have you ever chatted with people you didn't know? What did you talk about?

- Is there anyone online that you talk to on a regular basis but have never actually met?

After a few weeks, Eli felt that he knew almost everything about Michelle. They both loved airplanes, enjoyed hanging out at the mall with friends, and liked the same subjects in school. Michelle would even flirt with Eli. He wanted to ask Michelle if they could meet. But he worried about what his parents would think if he met up with someone from a chat room.

One afternoon, Eli decided to ask Michelle if they could get together. He took a deep breath, exhaled, and typed his message: "Hey Michelle, do you think we could meet next Thursday after school? You could come to my house." He hit send. He drummed his fingers on the table nervously as he waited for her response.

"That would be great! All I need is your address and I'll have my mom drop me off," read the message.

A smile stretched across Eli's face. He quickly typed in his address and told her they could meet at 4:00 p.m. next Thursday. The date was set. Eli logged off his computer as his dad walked through the door.

Think About It

- Have you ever given personal information to someone online? Why did you do it?

- What are some of the dangers of giving out personal information to someone you have never met in person? Do you think Eli thought about these dangers?

All Eli could think about at school on Thursday was his meeting with Michelle. The day seemed to drag on forever as he watched the clock. He was getting more and more excited with every passing minute.

At 3:00 p.m., he ran out of class and out of the school. Usually he took his time walking home so that he had a chance to talk more with his friends. But today he ran all the way home. He put gel in his hair, put on his coolest outfit, sprayed on a little of his dad's cologne, and waited for the clock to hit 4:00 p.m.

Eli stood at the window watching every car that drove by hoping it was Michelle. Shortly after 4:00 p.m., a blue car pulled up to the curb, the same color Michelle said her mom's car would be. But Eli's stomach dropped when a middle-aged man stepped out of the car and started walking toward his house. Suddenly, Eli realized Michelle wasn't a girl his age after all.

Think About It

- How would you react if you were in Eli's position?

- How would you feel if someone online lied to you?

- Do you think meeting someone you know only from the Internet is a good idea? Why do you believe that?

As Eli scrambled to collect his thoughts, he saw another car pull into the drive. It was Eli's dad, home from work early. When the man saw Eli's dad, he turned around quickly and ran toward his own car. He got in and took off.

"Eli, are you okay?" his dad asked as he entered the living room.

Suddenly, Eli realized Michelle wasn't a girl his age.

Tears formed in the corners of Eli's eyes. He was still trying to catch his breath. He nodded his head.

"Who was that man? What happened here?" his dad asked.

Eli's dad calmed him down and they sat on the couch to talk about the situation. Eli explained that he had been chatting with a person he thought was a girl his age and he arranged to meet her.

Eli's dad took a deep breath. "Eli, you're really lucky nothing happened to you," he said.

Eli's dad explained that many kids put themselves in danger every day by chatting with online predators and don't end up as lucky. He told his son that he could have been molested, kidnapped, or even killed.

"I'm going to call the police," Eli's dad said. "If you ever see this guy near the house again, call 911 immediately."

Eli just nodded. He was so embarrassed and just creeped out. How could he have believed that a middle-aged man was a girl who liked him?

Think About It

- what do you think could have happened if Eli's dad had not come home when he did?

- why do you think kids trust people they chat with online? Do you think they consider the dangers of chatting with strangers online?

- How can you be safer when you use the Internet?

The Internet can be a great tool for communication. You can chat with your friends from school or with people across the world. You can find chat rooms for people who share your interests. However, chatting on the Internet also brings some risks. It can put you in contact with people you would usually stay away from if you saw them on the street. It can also be easy to believe people are who they say they are.

It's important to remember to chat safely. Never give out any personal information on the Internet. Do not assume someone is a friend because he or she knows the name of your school or other personal information. Tell your parents or a trusted adult if anyone online says something that makes you nervous or uncomfortable or if someone asks you to meet in person.

Work It Out

1. Avoid chatting with people online whom you do not know in real life.

2. If you are chatting with a friend, be sure you receive the screen name directly from that person. An online predator can pretend to be one of your friends.

3. If you chat with someone you do not know in real life, do not give out any personal information, such as your name, school, address, or other landmarks near you.

4. Make sure your Facebook account has a privacy setting so that only people you know can view your profile.

5. Educate yourself on ways to avoid falling victim to an online predator. Share what you've learned with your friends so you can all enjoy the Web safely!

The Last Word from Brian

The Internet, as great as it is in so many aspects of life, has a dark side, too. Online predators are a real threat. Remember that it is always better to be safe than sorry. There is no reason why anyone online needs to know your personal information. Stay smart online and you'll stay safe, too!

6

Overexposed

Web sites with inappropriate content for kids have a strong presence on the Internet. One misspelled word in a search engine can often lead to a site filled with pornography. You might hear about pornography from TV shows, movies, or maybe even your friends and family and it might not seem like such a big deal. But, at your age, exposure to pornography can be damaging.

While you might be curious about the content of these sites, it is best to stay away from them. Michael was introduced to the world of inappropriate sites by accident. In the end, he wished he'd never seen them.

Michael's Story

Music from his favorite radio station played in the background as Michael was hard at work on the computer in the living room. He was doing a project for school that was due in a couple of weeks and wanted to get a head start. Michael was an honor student, and getting work done early was not out of the ordinary for him.

He went online and typed in a Web site that would give him useful information for his project. But he accidentally misspelled a word and a site that featured naked women filled his computer screen.

He knew he should just exit out of the page. His curiosity, however, got the best of him.

Michael was shocked. He knew he should just exit out of the page. His curiosity, however, got the best of him. He clicked to enter the site.

Michael looked at the photos of naked women on the page and even watched a couple of free video clips of couples engaging in sexual behavior. He clicked on links to several other sites. He had forgotten all about his project and spent the next hour looking at various inappropriate sites.

"Hey Michael?" his dad shouted as he walked through the front door. He was home from work. Caught off guard, Michael jumped out of his seat and quickly exited out of the sites before his dad walked into the living room.

"How's the project going? Are you going to get another A?" his dad asked.

"I just started," Michael stuttered. He could feel his face completely blushing. "I'll work on it again after school tomorrow."

Think About It

- why do you think Michael clicked to enter the web site? What would you do?

- Have you ever found inappropriate content on the Internet? Was it intentional or by accident?

Michael raced home after school the next day and quickly searched for other Web sites that featured porn. He liked looking at the pictures of naked women and decided he would print out a few to show off to his friends at school the next day. He thought they'd think it was really cool. He tucked the pictures into a folder and slipped it into his backpack.

Before the start of first period, Michael called a couple of his friends over to his locker. He opened up the folder and let them take a look at what was inside. His friend John looked embarrassed when he saw the pictures and walked away. His other friend Joseph seemed to like the pictures as much as Michael did and looked at every one of them. Joseph

thought it was cool that Michael had pictures of women barely dressed or not dressed at all.

"Where did you get these?" asked Joseph.

"Online," Michael said. "If you want to stop by after school, I'll show you." Michael knew his parents wouldn't be home until the evening.

"Awesome!" said Joseph.

Think About It

- what risks was Michael taking by bringing the pictures to school?

- why do you think one of Michael's friends wanted to look at the pictures and the other felt embarrassed?

Joseph came over to Michael's house after school to check out the Web sites. He brought a few of his friends that Michael didn't know. When they started looking at the Web sites, Joseph and his friends made some comments about the women in the photos that made Michael uncomfortable. He started to wish that he wasn't looking at the sites at all.

Joseph asked Michael to print out some pictures for him, so Michael hit the print button. He hoped Joseph and his friends would leave after that. Michael realized that he still had to finish his project, and he had decided that he didn't really like Joseph's other friends. Suddenly, Michael heard the front door open. His dad was home early! Michael frantically exited out of the Web sites, but the printer was still going.

Suddenly, Michael heard the front door open. His dad was home early!

Michael's dad was shocked when he saw what the boys were printing. Michael felt his face turn bright red. He wanted to dash out the door.

Michael's dad sent the others away instead. "You boys need to get home. Now."

Once they were gone he said, "Why are you looking at these pictures? Where did you find them?"

Michael explained how it had been a mistake at first.

"When we allow you to use the computer, we are trusting you to look at sites that are appropriate," Michael's father explained.

Michael looked at his feet. "Sorry," he said. Michael wished he would just be sent to his room already. He was humiliated to be talking about this with his dad.

Think About It

- Why do you think Joseph and his friends made Michael feel uncomfortable?

- How do you think Michael felt when his dad caught him looking at the web sites?

- What problems can arise from viewing inappropriate content on the web and having it in your possession?

At your age, it's natural to be curious about sex. When you are exposed to healthy sexual behavior it results in healthy sexual desires. If you are exposed to pornography, you can develop unhealthy and sometimes violent sexual desires.

Exposure to pornography can also shape attitudes and values toward relationships, intimacy, love, sex, and marriage. Internet pornography shows scenes of rape and often degrades women. Young boys who see these images might start to mistakenly believe it is okay to treat girls or women this way and in turn have sexual aggression problems in the future.

If you are curious about sex or have viewed inappropriate content online by accident or on purpose, talk to your parents about it and avoid looking at similar online content in the future. It can have a negative impact on your emotional and mental health. Plus, there are healthier ways to address this curiosity—talk with a trusted adult.

Work It Out

1. If an advertisement for a Web site containing inappropriate content

accidentally pops up on the computer, shut down the computer right away and restart. Attempting to click the ad off the screen may cause more ads and Web sites to pop up.

2. Use of filtering programs on your home computer can help you avoid viewing inappropriate or disturbing content altogether. Ask your parents if a filter program is installed on your computer.

3. Never attempt to guess how to type in a Web address. By doing that, you can avoid misspelling a word that could bring up an inappropriate Web site. Use a search engine instead of trying to type the site address into the address bar.

The Last Word from Brian

It can be embarrassing to end up on an inappropriate site. The best thing to do if it happens is exit out of the site as quickly as possible. These sites are only going to lead to trouble. While it is totally normal to be curious about the content of these sites, be careful of getting into things that can be damaging to you. Plus, by avoiding these sites, you're also avoiding some seriously embarrassing situations!

7

Left Out

Fitting in with your peers can be difficult and expensive if those same kids judge you by the technology you have—or don't have. Some kids have several high-tech devices, including cell phones, MP3 players, and handheld video games. Because having several high-tech gadgets has become the norm, it is easy to forget that there are kids who have few or none because their families choose to limit such purchases or they simply cannot afford them. You might be one of these guys.

If you don't have the things or brands that your friends have, it might make you feel left out or unaccepted by your peers. It can be pretty tough when you can't afford the technology that so many people enjoy. You might feel like everyone around you is better off than you are. You might even go to extremes to obtain devices that you are lacking. Connor took a huge risk to buy attention from his peers, but it didn't work out the way he planned.

Connor's Story

Most of the kids that attended school with Connor had the latest of everything. They were always talking about the newest phone coming out or the new game they wanted to get for their system. Anne, one of the girls in his group of friends, would bring articles to school from her dad's *MacWorld* magazine. At lunch, they'd read about the newest gadgets that were coming out.

Anne knew everything about technology and Connor learned a lot from her. She was the coolest girl he knew. When they talked about

Fitting in with your peers can be difficult and expensive if those same kids judge you by the technology you have—or don't have.

cool computers and cell phones, Connor usually pretended he had all of those things. But he was sure Anne and his other friends noticed when he didn't come to school rocking out to an MP3 player or whip out a cell phone when the last bell rang.

Connor's family couldn't afford the latest high-tech products. Their television was tiny, and they

didn't even have a game system. There was only one computer in the house, and it was clunky and old. No one in Connor's family even had a cell phone. Connor thought his friends would laugh if they found out about the reality of his situation. And he could only imagine what Anne would say!

One night after school, he asked his parents if he could have the latest version of an MP3 player for his birthday. He knew it was a long shot, but it was the only thing he wanted that year.

"Connor, I'm sorry, but you know we can't afford that right now," his mom said. "Money is tight now, but maybe someday we can get one for you."

A frown stretched across Connor's face. He understood the reason, but it definitely didn't make things easier. "I know. I know," Connor said, his voice soaked in disappointment. "It would just be so awesome to have one . . ."

Connor sat on his bed that night and thought about how badly he wanted an MP3 player. He just *had* to have one! He was so tired of never having anything.

Think About It

- Did you ever feel like an outsider because you didn't have the stuff that all your friends had?

- Were you ever teased because you couldn't afford to buy the newest MP3 player or the newest video game?

- Have you ever asked your parents if you could have an expensive item even though you knew they couldn't afford to buy it? How did you feel when they said no?

Then, a thought popped into his head. Perhaps he could steal one. His friend Tommy stole candy bars from the gas station all the time and he'd never been caught. Connor knew that stealing an MP3 player might be more difficult and that he could get in a lot of trouble if he got caught. But he couldn't help but think about how cool it would be to have one. Anne would be impressed, and he wouldn't feel like he was someone who faded into the background at school. Connor decided he was going to steal an MP3 player at the mall that weekend.

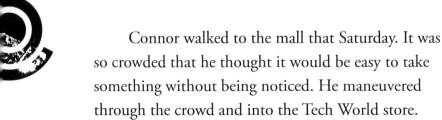

Think About It

• Have you ever thought about stealing something? why did you want to steal it?

• How important is it for you to fit in at school? Do you feel like you need to have the latest high-tech gadgets in order to fit in?

Connor walked to the mall that Saturday. It was so crowded that he thought it would be easy to take something without being noticed. He maneuvered through the crowd and into the Tech World store. He walked over to the display of MP3 players and spotted the one he wanted.

"Can I help you with something?" a salesman said as he walked up behind Connor.

Connor was startled and jumped as he heard the voice. "I'm good," Connor said. "I'm just looking around while my parents finish up some shopping."

The salesman smiled and walked over to another customer. Connor now had an opening to make his move. He took a deep breath, shook off his nerves, and slipped the MP3 player into his pocket. Tiny beads of sweat formed on his forehead as he walked slowly toward the store exit.

Connor picked up his pace as he headed to the mall exit, but as soon as he stepped outside, a security guard stopped him. Connor froze.

"Come with me, son," the guard said, clapping a hand on Connor's shoulder.

Connor was frightened and embarrassed as he walked with the security guard through the crowded mall. People were looking at him. What were his parents going to say? Would he have to go to jail?

Then, out of the corner of his eye, he saw Anne walking with some of her friends. She stopped and smiled when she saw Connor. But as her eyes moved to the security guard next to him, she frowned. Connor was so embarrassed. He realized he'd just let everyone down. This was not the impression he'd wanted to make on Anne.

People were looking at him. What were his parents going to say? Would he have to go to jail?

Think About It

- Have you ever been caught stealing something? Do you know anyone who's stolen something?

- Would you feel humiliated if you were caught doing something wrong in public?

- How do you think Connor felt when he saw Anne? What do you think Connor's parents will do when they find out he stole something?

Not being able to afford the same high-tech gadgets as your classmates can make you feel stressed out. You may feel as if you don't fit in or can't keep up because of your family's financial situation. That kind of pressure can lead to anxiety. If you fear being around your peers or feel inferior to them because of that situation, talk to your parents about it. This is important because, if anxiety is left to sit inside you, it can affect your ability to communicate, your performance in school, and how you relate to others.

You know that stealing is not the right way to solve any problems. Some kids feel justified in stealing because their parents cannot afford to buy them things. Others might think that since the store makes so much money, they won't even notice one missing item. But stealing is a crime and making yourself a criminal won't earn you any respect from your friends.

Work It Out

1. Be creative. If you don't have an MP3 player to play songs on, try writing a song or play an instrument. If you don't have a video game system, come up with a cool game to play with your friends in the

neighborhood, play a sport, or play video games at a friend's house. Or, see if one of your friends has an old system that they're willing to give you or sell cheap.

2. Try to purchase gadgets yourself. You can do jobs for people your parents know and trust in the neighborhood. Being able to buy what you want by saving for it feels even better than someone getting it for you.

3. Rather than worry about what you don't have, focus on the good things in your life that you do have.

4. Don't base your self-worth on what you have or don't have. Base it on who you are as a person.

The Last Word from Brian

You may have felt socially unaccepted at some point in your life. And perhaps it was because you didn't have the coolest game system or your parents refused to get you a cell phone. But not having the latest high-tech toys shouldn't be a deciding factor in how we are judged by our peers or how we feel about ourselves. Material items mean little in the grand scheme of things. By being kind to others and finding things you have in common with them, you can still fit in socially and have healthy friendships. You don't need something that runs on batteries to make that happen.

8
Cyberbully

You have probably had some type of experience with a bully by this time in your life. Most likely the bullying you witnessed was done on a school playground or in the lunchroom. But technological advances have taken bullying a step further. Bullies can now prey on their victims online. This is known as cyberbullying.

Bullies are often insecure about themselves and attempt to remedy the problem by putting down others. With access to the Internet, cyberbullies can do this in a cruel manner through instant messages or e-mails. They will attack their victims' personal appearance, insult their intelligence, or maybe force them to quit an activity they love, such as a sports team. A bully's actions over an extended period of time can cause the victim to suffer severe psychological or emotional damage. And no matter how tough and confident you are, a cyberbully can really affect your life. Nick learned firsthand how to handle a cyberbully.

Bullies are often insecure about themselves and attempt to remedy the problem by putting down others.

Nick's Story

Nick wasn't from a family with a lot of money. He had four siblings and money was stretched pretty tight. Most of the time he wore hand-me-down clothes from his older brothers because his parents couldn't afford new stuff for everyone each school year.

Think About It

- Are you from a family where money is tight? Do people tease you about it?

- Have you ever had to wear hand-me-down clothes? Did it bother you?

- How do you think Nick feels about his family?

- Have you ever teased someone because of his or her clothes or material possessions?

It didn't bother Nick much to be in that situation because he had an intense drive to make his life better in the long run. He set high goals for himself. He worked hard in school and was a talented soccer player who always practiced hard and gave his best effort in every game. His dream was to get an academic or athletic scholarship for college.

At home one night, Nick was on the family computer chatting with a few of his friends. He received an instant message from Jared. Jared was a kid on the soccer team. Nick was a little surprised to hear from Jared because they never talked too much.

"You really need to work on your game, man. Watching you practice tonight was hilarious!" the message from Jared read. "And what were you wearing? Don't you have any cooler soccer shorts than those old raggedy things?" another read.

Nick didn't reply. He was surprised that Jared would be so harsh. Jared was a pretty quiet kid at school.

Then another message came in. "You know most people who talk to you at school are just pretending to like you, and we laugh about it later, cuz it's so funny how you think you have so many friends! You should just quit the team and save yourself the embarrassment!"

Nick pretended what Jared had said didn't bother him. "Whatever, man," he wrote. "I don't believe anything you are saying!" Nick logged off

and went to bed, but he couldn't stop thinking about
what Jared had said about him.

Think About It

- Have people you know ever teased you over the
  Internet?

- How would you feel if you received messages
  like Nick did?

- Have you ever teased someone over
  the Internet?

Eventually, Nick fell asleep and forgot about Jared's comments by morning. That day at school, he walked past Jared and a few soccer players who all looked at him and laughed. Nick didn't know what they were laughing about, but he worried they were laughing at him.

That night, Jared instant messaged Nick again. He continued to tell him how he had no athletic skill and that he should just give up. Jared told him he was crazy to think he'd get a scholarship to play soccer. Some of Jared's friends also started messaging Nick about the same types of things.

The next day at school Nick decided to confront Jared about the messages. He found Jared alone at his locker right before soccer practice.

"Hey Jared!" Nick called. Jared pretended not to hear him, so Nick ran over.

"What's going on?" Nick asked. "Why are you and your friends being such jerks to me online?"

Jared didn't say anything. Nick was confused. Jared had seemed so tough online. But now, he was a total wimp.

"Seriously, knock it off. What did I ever do to you?" Nick said.

"It's not my fault if you can't take a little criticism," Jared mumbled. "Chill." He walked away.

Think About It

• Do you think it was a good idea for Nick to confront Jared? What are some other ways he could've handled the situation?

• Why does Jared seem like a "total wimp?"

Nick hoped his conversation with Jared would put an end to the cyberbullying. Unfortunately, that night he received an instant message from Jared's friend Rich.

"Stop bugging Jared," Rich wrote. "You're such a loser. You should be careful what you say to us. Don't bother him again!"

Rich's message made Nick feel really uneasy. For days afterward, he couldn't stop thinking about it. In the meantime, Jared and his friends continued to send instant messages to Nick and make fun of him. Sometimes Jared or Rich sent him nasty e-mails, too.

During soccer practice, Rich and Jared never said anything to Nick, but Nick felt really uncomfortable around them. He kept messing up his shots and passes. After a few weeks, he decided to quit the team.

Nick's coach was upset to hear Nick was quitting. Nick used to be the team's star player. Nick's coach asked the school's guidance counselor, Mr. Washington, to have a talk with Nick.

So, one morning, Mr. Washington called Nick down to his office.

"You quit the soccer team. Your grades have dropped, too," said Mr. Washington. "What's going on? You used to be such a great student."

Nick didn't say anything. He was worried that if he did, Jared would find out and things would get worse.

But Mr. Washington kept asking questions. "Why did you quit the team? You were one of the best players."

Nick took a deep breath. He hated the way his life was going. He knew he had to tell Mr. Washington what was going on. Maybe it would help. "Some guys have been giving me crap,"

Nick said. "But, it's not really a huge deal," he quickly added.

"Well," said Mr. Washington, "why don't you tell me about it anyway?"

Mr. Washington sat back in his chair and listened as Nick talked about everything that had happened to him. His counselor pointed out that by giving up on school and soccer, he was letting the cyberbullies get the best of him. He told Nick he was doing exactly what the bullies wanted.

"These guys are crossing the line," Mr. Washington explained. "And, you have too much going for you to let them mess it up. It's time to get the principal, and maybe the police, involved."

Think About It

- If a school counselor approached you about a problem, would you be willing to open up to him or her the way Nick did?

- Do you think things will get better for Nick now? What kind of punishment do you think Nick's bullies deserve?

Cyberbullies are becoming a big problem for many adolescents. A cyberbully will attack you in various ways, including the use of gossip or by sending you intimidating messages and threats. Cyberbullying is serious, and it's important to get it under control quickly to avoid emotional damage and stress in your life.

Cyberbullies are usually bullying because they are having some trouble in their own lives. It is not your fault that you are being bullied. If a cyberbully is bothering you, talk to your parents or an adult you trust right away about the problem. Keeping your feelings inside and allowing the cyberbully to continue to harass you is only going to make matters worse for you in the long run. By taking a stand early on, you will be able to get past the cyberbullying and move on with your life.

Work It Out

1. Don't respond to the messages you receive from a cyberbully. Instead, remain calm and walk away from the computer if necessary. A cyberbully wants your attention. If you don't give it to him, you win the battle.

2. If a cyberbully is harassing you on a consistent basis or threatens you, don't be afraid to talk to someone who can help.

3. Make sure you save every message you receive from a cyberbully. The more information you save, the more evidence you will have if you need to report the cyberbullying to an adult or other authorities.

4. Talk to your parents about blocking e-mails and instant messages from a cyberbully.

5. Don't become a cyberbully yourself. Before you send any instant message, text message, or e-mail, read over it one more time. Make sure you aren't cyberbullying!

The Last Word from Brian

The best thing you can do if someone decides to cyberbully you is to ignore him and let someone you trust know about it immediately. Often, cyberbullies will target more than one victim. If you are being bullied, there is a good chance other kids are suffering from the same cyberbully. Your speaking out against a cyberbully might help many other kids. Remember, the world can be tough to deal with. Try to build people up—not tear them down.

9

Stuntman

All of us have probably seen someone perform a crazy stunt in an Internet video. Popular sites such as YouTube are full of acts that can put you or others in danger. Some kids like to imitate the stunts they see online. They might even post their own video of the stunt online to show off to their friends. Many of these videos post no warnings about not trying these stunts at home, and if they do, many viewers just ignore them. Sometimes it becomes a game for guys to dare each other to do something even more dangerous the next time.

However, these stunts can be really dangerous, even life threatening.

Something that looks like a lot of fun can quickly turn into a trip to the hospital. Take it from Craig. He learned just how dangerous imitating a stunt could be.

Craig's Story

Craig waited patiently in front of his computer as a video of a wild skateboard stunt loaded

Popular sites such as YouTube are full of acts that can put you or others in danger.

onto his monitor. Once it appeared on the screen, he quickly hit play. The teenager featured in the stunt skated down his driveway as quickly as he could and attempted to ollie over a friend who was lying on the ground. He managed to successfully make the jump, although the back wheels on his skateboard did graze his friend's stomach as he landed.

Craig couldn't believe the skater pulled off the jump. He thought to himself that it would be so cool if he could execute a spectacular stunt similar to the one he had just seen. After all, Craig was a pretty decent skater, and it seemed easy enough.

Watching skateboard stunt videos was a daily routine for Craig. The more he watched, the more eager he became to attempt a stunt. He told his friends over and over again how cool it would be if he could pull off a jaw-dropping trick on his skateboard. The problem was that he could never build up enough courage to go for it.

Craig changed his mind one day when he heard a skater from down the block had perfected a stunt he had seen online. He even posted it on YouTube. Craig decided it was time to overcome his fear and attempt a stunt. He found one online that he thought he could do. The skater in the video slid down a really steep, metal railing. Craig had never tried that trick before, but he'd always wanted to. He knew of a railing in the park that was even taller than the one the skater in the video had used. Craig thought it would be awesome if he could pull it off.

That afternoon, Craig texted his friend Aaron and told him to bring his camera with him when they met up to go skateboarding on Saturday morning.

Think About It

- Why do you think Craig wants to perform this stunt? Do you think he will be successful? Why or why not?

- Do you believe that you could impress your friends by doing a stunt you saw online?

- Do you think it would be cool to post a video of yourself online performing a dangerous stunt?

Craig met Aaron at the park on Saturday morning.

"This is gonna be sweet!" Aaron said as he positioned himself near the metal railing. Craig just nodded and strapped on his helmet.

Craig skated over to the edge of the sidewalk, gripped his skateboard in his sweaty hands, and took a deep breath. Aaron had the video camera in his hand aimed at Craig. Craig started to have second thoughts, but a couple of other skaters had gathered around to watch the stunt.

"What's he doing?" one older guy asked Aaron as he approached.

"Just wait," Aaron said. "It's gonna be awesome."

Craig took a deep breath. He pushed off against the sidewalk with his foot as he picked up speed and glided toward the railing. Just before he reached the stairway, he ollied his board into the air and slid awkwardly down the rail. For a minute he felt like he might actually pull it off. But, suddenly, Craig lost his balance and fell hard to the cement.

Craig screamed loudly as he hit the ground. Blood flowed from a cut on his chin, and pain rushed through his body. He couldn't believe how much he hurt. He tried to stop crying as Aaron leaned over him, yelling, "Dude! Are you okay?" Aaron sounded panicked, and Craig couldn't even move, it hurt so bad. Next thing he knew, Aaron had called an ambulance and Craig was being taken to the hospital.

Think About It

- If Craig didn't have any friends around watching him, do you think he still would have tried the stunt?

- Have you ever suffered an injury because you tried to imitate something you saw in an online video?

At the hospital, Craig got stitches for his cut. He also found out that he had broken a couple of ribs, his right arm, and two of his fingers.

Craig's doctor came in to explain to him how to take care of his wounds. Before he left, the doctor turned and said, "Listen, kid, you were really lucky. Just last week I saw a kid who tried to do a stunt on

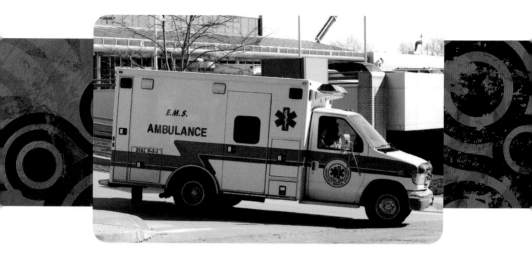

a skateboard just like you and now he's in a coma. If you hadn't been wearing a helmet you could be in the same shape. Some kids die doing that stuff."

Craig realized how lucky he was to have gotten off with only broken bones. He lay in a hospital bed thinking about how dumb it was to do something so dangerous. He wasn't going to be able to skateboard again for a long time. He was also going to miss a concert that weekend. He wondered if there was a way to warn others so they wouldn't make the same mistake he did.

After he left the hospital, Craig decided he was going to post the video of him attempting the stunt. Only, at the end of the video, he would have Aaron film him discussing the dangers of attempting stupid things that you see online. Craig believed it was the best thing he could do—and he hoped others would learn from his terrible mistake.

It's normal to want to fit in and do something that your friends will think is cool. Most kids your age are striving to be individuals, but in all reality, you are in an age group where most kids are likely to act the way others do. If a group of friends you hang out with decides to attempt a crazy stunt, you may be more than willing to get in on the act. Stop and think about the consequences of your actions.

You may enjoy watching videos of stunts done by your favorite skateboarder or BMX rider. Because you idolize that person, you may think it's okay to try the same stunt. But the professional athletes who do these tricks are trained to attempt daring stunts, and even then, there is no guarantee they will avoid an injury.

Work It Out

1. Remember that usually if the trick looks very hard to do, it is probably being done by professional stuntmen who are trained in what they do and do it for a living. Work on your basic skills now, and maybe someday you'll be experienced enough to become a stuntman yourself!

2. Think about the consequences of attempting to imitate something you saw online. Think about how badly you could injure yourself and how you and your parents would feel if you did injure yourself.

3. If you want to make a video of yourself, try something that won't cause any harm to yourself or others, such as attempting to make a trick shot with a basketball.

4. No matter what sport you are playing or how minor your tricks, always wear protective gear such as a helmet and pads.

The Last Word from Brian

Once, I was dumb enough to ride a skateboard down a hill with my hands in my pockets. I hit a crack in the road, flew off my board, and chipped a tooth. I also needed stitches for my chin. Trust me, it's not worth your time to imitate a stunt that an amateur was crazy enough to attempt or that a professional stuntman performed. By doing it, you are only putting yourself at risk for a serious injury.

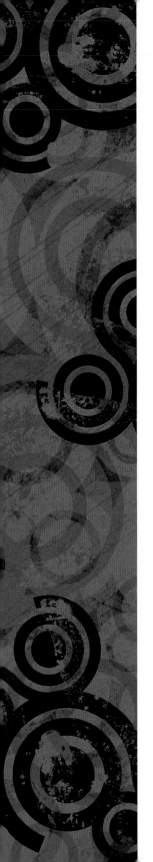

10
Public Matter

How often do you use text messages? Many guys your age text all the time. You might send text messages to your friends, girlfriend, siblings, and parents. If you happen to see something cool or hilarious, it's great to be able to snap a picture with your cell phone and send it to all your friends.

Over the last few years, this form of communication has been taken to a new and inappropriate level. It is known as sexting. Sexting is the act of sending sexual messages or photos electronically. Most of the time, it is done on cell phones. Sam experimented with sexting when he met his first girlfriend. When

the relationship ended, he learned the hard way that
his actions had serious consequences.

Sam's Story

Sam and Jessica had been dating for a few months,
and like many preteens, they were tempted to explore
their relationship from a sexual standpoint. One
night Sam was in his
room and thought about   *Sexting is the act of*
how surprised Jessica   *sending sexual messages or*
would be if he sent her   *photos electronically.*
a seminaked picture of
himself. He took off his shirt, snapped a picture with
his phone, typed up a quick message that contained
sexual content, and hit send.

Jessica sent a text message back in a few minutes. It said, "Wanna C a hot pic of me?"

"Definitely!" Sam replied.

A few minutes later, Sam received a picture of Jessica with her shirt off. He thought she looked amazing. Sam called Jessica. He told her they should show off more of their bodies. Jessica told him she would think about it.

Think About It

- Have you ever tried sexting someone or do you know people at school who engage in sexting?

- Would you feel awkward sending a seminaked picture of yourself to someone you're dating?

- How would you feel if someone you were dating sent a seminaked picture to you?

Sam told a couple of his friends at school about how he and Jessica had exchanged pictures of themselves. He talked about going even further with the sexting. His friend Joe warned him that you could get in serious trouble for doing something like that.

"I don't know if I'd keep doing it," Joe said. "I heard something about it on the news. A kid got in trouble with the cops for sending a picture of his junk to girls in his class."

97

Sam shrugged off his friend's remarks. "Don't worry," Sam said. "The pictures are going to stay between Jessica and me. We won't let anyone else see them."

After school, Sam went home and got completely naked. He took pictures of himself and sent the pictures to Jessica. He included a message that read, "It's your turn now!"

A few minutes later, Jessica sent some pictures of her naked body to Sam. Sam and Jessica sent a few more pictures back and forth. They often included sexually explicit messages with the pictures.

Think About It

- If you were warned that sexting could get you into serious trouble, would you blow off the warning the way Sam did?

- If you received a naked picture, would you keep it to yourself or send it to others?

A few weeks later, Jessica and Sam got into a big fight and he broke up with her. Jessica was really mad about it. "You'll regret this! You're such a jerk!" she yelled.

The next day at school, Sam heard that Jessica had sent a couple of the pictures he'd sent to her

to her friends. Now it seemed like all the girls were laughing at him as he walked down the halls.

Sam was angry and embarrassed. He couldn't believe Jessica would do something like that! When Sam got home from school that day he uploaded the pictures of Jessica onto his computer and printed them out. He was going to bring them to school and pass them out to his friends.

Now it seemed like all the girls were laughing at him as he walked down the halls.

The next day Sam was walking down the hallway to his locker with the folder of Jessica's pictures in his hand. He saw his favorite teacher, Mr. Stokes, walking in his direction. Sam wanted to say hello to Mr. Stokes before class started, so he quickly tried to catch him. Just as he approached Mr. Stokes, the folder slipped out of his hand. Jessica's pictures were thrown from the folder and drifted to the floor of the hallway.

Sam's face turned beet red as he looked into the face of someone he admired so much. Mr. Stokes looked shocked. He sent Sam to the office. Sam knew he was in a ton of trouble.

Think About It

- How could Sam have handled this situation without stooping to Jessica's level?

- What kind of punishment do you think Sam is going to get?

Sexting has grown more popular among tweens and teens in recent years. Sexting is used to send a sexual image or explicit message to a boyfriend, girlfriend, or even someone you would like to date in the future.

The problem is that sexting can have serious and lasting consequences. The image is often forwarded to others and can result in embarrassment for the person who sent the original image or message. The image or message can be used against you by others, and can cause you to feel humiliated around your peers.

Sexting can also lead to legal trouble and put a dent in your future. The damage can be permanent. Creating, transmitting, and even possessing a nude, seminude, or sexually explicit image of a minor can be considered child pornography. Punishments range from paying a fine to having to register as a sex offender. The consequences connected to sexting are drastic, and it is best to think twice before you hit send.

Work It Out

1. Work on developing a positive self-image. If you have good self-esteem, you will be less

likely to need approval from others, which is sometimes the root of sexting.

2. Learn about what sexting is and the harm it can do to you. Understand that any pictures you send could become public for anyone to see. Also remember that for underage kids, it is illegal to send these pictures.

3. Don't give in to the pressure you may feel from a peer to show off an intimate part of your body. You shouldn't have to do something you're not comfortable with to make someone like you.

The Last Word from Brian

Sexting may seem as if it's no big deal if the pictures are kept between two people. However, the odds are that other people will get their hands on them. The scary thing is those pictures could end up in the possession of strangers and could haunt you into adulthood. So, if you want to express your feelings to a girl you like, find a more positive and subtle way to do it. The risk that comes with sexting someone just isn't worth the headache.

Technology has been around for as long as you can remember, and while it certainly serves a purpose in this ever-changing, fast-paced world of ours, knowing how and when to use it properly is not always easy. There is nothing wrong with having the power of technology at your fingertips. Just don't view it as being as vital to life as breathing. If you happen to make a mistake in your use of a high-tech gadget, remember that no one is perfect. Live and learn from your mistake and keep moving forward.

Perhaps you already have or will have a cell phone at some point in the future. There is nothing wrong with using it to make a call or send a text message, but avoid using it to cheat on a test or for sexting. Taking that route will only lead to problems. Don't believe that you always need to have the latest and greatest when it comes to high-tech gadgets or gaming systems. You don't need the best of everything to fit in socially. So, be someone who appreciates the high-tech gadgets that you have and don't put down others who may not be as fortunate as you. Avoid using technology in ways that put you in dangerous situations.

Keep the information you have learned from this book on your mind. It will prove helpful now and in the future. Technology is important and it always will be. It will continue to move you forward and improve your life. As long as you remember to use technology in healthy and positive ways, the possibilities are endless.

TTYL,

Brian

Remember, a healthful life is about balance. Now that you know how to walk that path, pay it forward to a friend or even yourself! Remember the Work It Out tips throughout this book, and then take these steps to get healthy and get going.

- Don't allow technology to consume your life. Designate times for it.

- When you are online, do not give out personal information. Never agree to meet someone you talk to only online.

- Tell yourself you don't need to impress your peers to make them your friends. True friends will like you regardless of what gadgets you have.

- If you are feeling unhappy with your life, talk to someone. Get the help you need to get healthy rather than closing up and only talking to people online.

- Use your cell phone responsibly and follow the rules. Don't allow the temptation to cheat or disregard school policy rule you.

- If you are a victim of cyberbullying or any type of bullying, tell someone. Don't try to handle it yourself, and don't let it change who you are.

- Stick to video games that are age appropriate. Limit your game play to allow time for your friends and doing things outside your home.

- While imitating stunts seen online may seem like a good way to impress your friends, remember these actions can have dangerous consequences. You can seriously injure yourself or even die. Leave these stunts to the professionals and don't put yourself at risk.

- Be responsible when you are online. Make the choice to turn away from Web sites and images that your parents wouldn't approve of and that, in your gut, you know are inappropriate. Remind yourself of the long-term psychological effects viewing inappropriate Web sites and images can have on you.

- Stay away from sexting. The long-term consequences of it can be devastating. The pictures you send through sexting will likely end up in the hands of more than just one person, and that can lead to embarrassment and can even have legal repercussions.

Additional Resources

Selected Bibliography

Courtney, Vicki. *Logged On and Tuned Out: A Non-Techie's Guide to Parenting a Tech-Savvy Generation.* Nashville, TN: B&H Publishing, 2007.

Dutwin, David. *Unplug Your Kids: A Parent's Guide to Raising Happy, Active and Well-Adjusted Children in the Digital Age.* Avon, MA: Adams Media, 2009.

Espejo, Roman. *Should Social Networking Sites Be Banned? (At Issue Series).* Detroit, MI: Greenhaven Press, 2008.

Kelsey, Candice M. *Generation My Space: Helping Your Teen Survive Online Adolescence.* New York: Da Capo Press, 2007.

Palfrey, John. *Born Digital: Understanding the First Generation of Digital Natives.* New York: Basic Books, 2008.

Further Reading

Jakubiak, David J. *A Smart Kid's Guide to Avoiding Online Predators.* New York: Rosen Publishing Group, 2009.

Jakubiak, David J. *A Smart Kid's Guide to Social Networking Online.* New York: Rosen Publishing Group, 2009.

MacEachern, Robyn. *Cyber Bullying Deal With It and Ctrl Alt Delete It.* Toronto, Canada: Lorimer, James and Company, Limited, 2009.

Willard, Nancy. *Cyber-Safe Kids, Cyber-Savvy Teens: Helping Young People Learn to Use the Internet Safely and Responsibly.* San Francisco, CA: Jossey-Bass. 2007.

Web Sites

To learn more about using technology responsibly, visit ABDO Publishing Company online at **www.abdopublishing.com**. Web sites about using technology responsibly are featured on our Book Links page. These links are routinely monitored and updated to provide the most current information available.

For More Information

For more information on this subject, contact or visit the following organizations:

Boy Scouts of America
1325 W. Walnut Hill Lane, Irving, TX 75015
972-580-2000
www.scouting.org
The Boy Scouts, a values-based youth development organization, has been around for 100 years. The organization provides an opportunity for children to enjoy a variety of outdoor activities and have fun outside the cyberworld.

i-Safe
5900 Pasteur Court, Suite #100, Carlsbad, CA 92008
760-603-7911
isafe.org
The i-Safe program is designed to provide students with the information they need in order to safely navigate through the Internet and avoid behavior that can have a negative impact on their lives. Founded in 1998, i-Safe is in all 50 states.

Glossary

addiction
The state of being overly dependent on something.

anxiety
A relatively permanent state of worry and nervousness, usually accompanied by attacks of panic.

cyberbullying
The use of the Internet to harass or bully others.

fine
An amount of money you pay as punishment for breaking the law.

gaming
The playing of video games using game systems and a television screen.

imitate
To copy the actions, appearance, mannerisms, or speech of another; mimicking.

inappropriate
Not suited to a given purpose or circumstance.

obsession
To be consumed by something so much that it takes over your life.

secluded
Alone and away from society.

sexting

The act of sending sexually explicit messages or photos with a cell phone.

sexual predator

A person who preys upon others and wants to harm them sexually.

tendency

The likelihood that something will or may happen.

Index

anxiety, 74

blogs, 40, 43, 46

cell phones, 10–19, 20, 31–37, 67, 68, 94–97, 100–101
    school rules, 12, 17, 18–19
    text messaging, 10, 13, 19, 95–96, 97
chat rooms, 49, 56
cheating, 10–19
counselors, 82–83, 85
cyberbullies, 76–85

e-mail, 82

Facebook, 40–41, 43, 46, 57
filter programs, 65
fitting in, 66–72, 74–75

instant messaging, 42, 43–44, 45, 49–51, 78–79, 80–82, 85

MP3 player, 68–71, 75

online friends, 41–42, 45, 47
online predators, 45–46, 55, 56–57

parents, 19, 29, 38–39, 47, 56, 64–65, 74–75, 84–85, 93
pornography, 58–65, 100
privacy settings, 57

sexting, 94–101
shyness, 41, 46
social networking, 40
stealing, 70–72, 74–75
stunt videos, 86–93

video camera, 88, 89
video games, 20–29
    addiction, 28–29
    ratings, 21, 28
    violence, 21–22, 24–27, 28–29

YouTube, 86, 88

About the Author

Brian Lester was born and raised in Rockford, Illinois. As a sports writer, he has covered athletics at every level, from high school to the pros, and has spent the last eight years covering the University of Findlay for *The Courier* in Findlay, Ohio. He was named the best sports writer in Virginia in the non-daily newspaper category in 1998 and has won two Associated Press Awards in Ohio.

Photo Credits

Elnur Amikishiyev/Bigstock, 12; Robert Payne/iStockphoto, 15, 22; Vlad Mereuta/Fotolia, 16; Charles Knox/Bigstock, 26; Catherine Yeulet/iStockphoto, 32; Mark Lennihan/AP Images, 35; Catherine Yeulet/Bigstock, 36, 95; Tan Kian Khoon/Fotolia, 41; Stephan Hoerold/iStockphoto, 44; Getty Images, 51; Fotolia, 52, 54; Darko Novakovic/Bigstock, 61; Michael Chamberlin/Bigstock, 63; Stas Perov/Fotolia, 68; iStockphoto, 71, 98; Svetlana Khvorostova/Bigstock, 73; Jim Kolaczko/iStockphoto, 79; Galina Barskaya/Bigstock, 80; Nicholas Rjabow/Bigstock, 89; Robert Pernell/Fotolia, 91